My Little Occult Book Club

A Creepy Collection

Steven Rhodes

CHRONICLE BOOKS

SAN FRANCISCO

Book Club Order Form

Ordering Information:
Please indicate how many of each item you would like to purchase.

GIVE ORDER FORM AND
MONEY TO CULT LEADER BY

STUDENT'S NAME

NAME ....

ADDRESS ....

CITY ....

STATE .... ZIP ....

CATALOG

**OVER 45 BOOKS
TO ORDER!**
★★★

Book Club Order Form (Cont.)

MY LITTLE OCCULT BOOK CLUB
666 Doomsday Parade, Crypt Valley, USA

Total Items

Total Cost

DELIVERED RIGHT TO YOUR DOOR!

Introduction

Dear Boys and Girls,

Can you believe it's that time again already? You're holding in your hands the latest edition of the **My Little Occult Book Club catalog!** Within these pages you'll find hours and hours of super summer reading, as well as activities, puzzles, games, and crafts! It's jam-packed!

In this bumper issue we're thrilled to bring you more of your old favorites, including the **Demon Summoning** book series, while also offering some brand new titles like **Let's Conjure Bloody Mary** and **Death Metal Sing-Along!** And don't worry firebugs—we haven't forgotten about you either with the long awaited second edition of **Advanced Pyrokinesis**. Incinerate those troubles away, kids!

In addition to the always popular activity books and teen novels, we're also proud to present some cult-tastic exclusive mail-order products! Be the envy of your coven by owning your very own **Cursed Videocassette**. You could even go on an intergalactic adventure with our **Alien-Attracting Helmet!**

The occult calendar is a hive of activity this quarter. As the planets enter the Zorloff cycle, it signals the arrival of our interdimensional overlords and the end of our time here on Planet Earth. As we hurtle relentlessly toward the apocalyptic end-days, what better time to catch up on the latest reading lists and get our affairs in order?

So fill out your order forms today, and hand them in to your Cult Leader or High Priestess.

Very soon books, activities, and more will be on their way to your doorstep. We even have **Bonus Prizes** for multiple orders, so what are you waiting for? Send those forms in now!

As always, everyone here at the My Little Occult Book Club headquarters would like to sincerely thank you all for your continued membership! Remember, unsubscribing is not an option, and you are all sworn to secrecy. Keeping dark secrets is fun!

Dust off your robes, light some candles, find a nice quiet place—like a haunted graveyard, a burned-out church, or an ancient cursed forest—and HAPPY READING!

Until we meet again.
Your friend (and book club editor),
Steven Rhodes

(P.S. I know I usually ask you to write and tell me what books you like best, but this time don't bother. With the inevitable demise of the planet and our transformation into our final bodily forms, it would be a futile exercise.)

*Note to Parents: Here in the mailroom we've received several complaints suggesting that our books aren't suitable for children. Please be assured that we have read your letters carefully and have destroyed them all in a ritualistic blood ceremony.

AND SO MUCH MORE INSIDE!

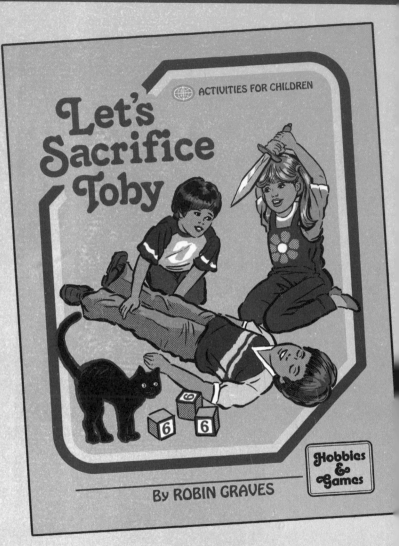

ACTIVITIES FOR CHILDREN

Let's Sacrifice Toby

Hobbies & Games

BY ROBIN GRAVES

Let's Sacrifice Toby

by Robin Graves 42 pages

"Quit your squabbling and play nicely together! Mommy's having a nervous breakdown!" screamed Mikey, Sarah, and Toby's mother. But this wasn't what she had in mind!

In a desperate bid to extend their school vacation, the Henderson kids make a bold plea to the **Dark Gods of Summer Break.** But miracles like this demand a sacrifice.

They must offer Toby's earthly soul in exchange for an extra two weeks of summer. "That seems like a fair trade," Toby thought. What could go wrong?

Learn about the power of cooperation, bargaining, and human sacrifice with this step-by-step activity book.
(Sacrificial dagger not included)

~~$4.50~~ **$2.95**

SPECIAL VALUE!

9

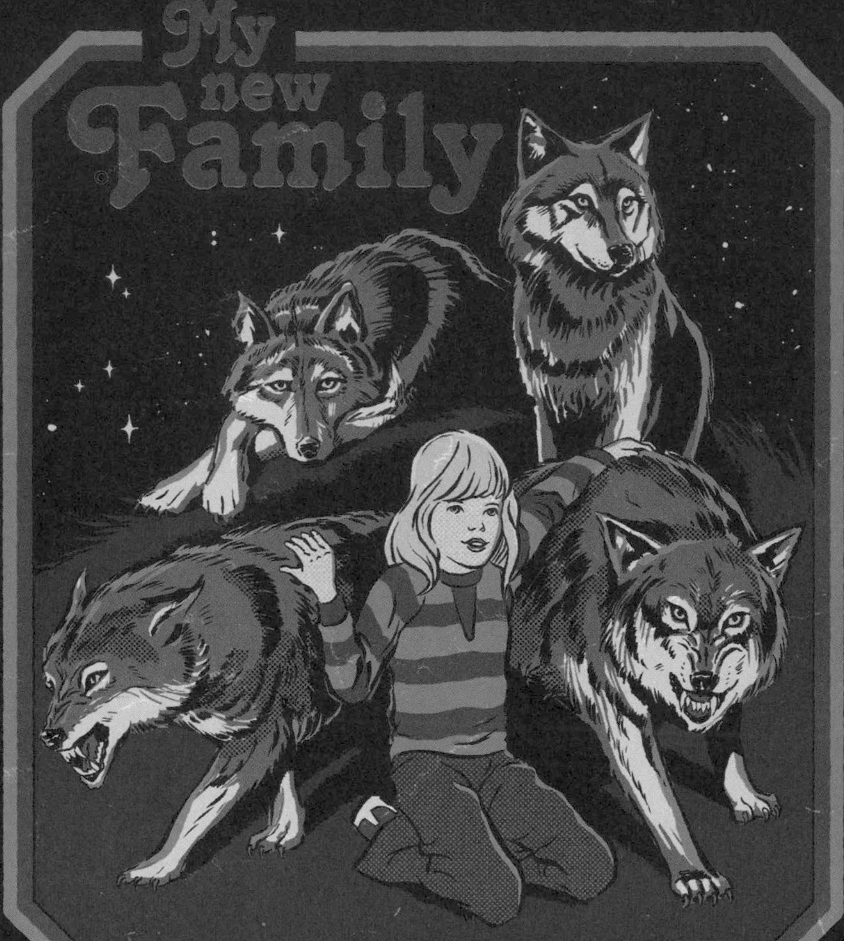
My new Family

Let's Dig for Treasure

ACTIVITIES FOR CHILDREN

JOIN THE DOTS

Connect all the dots to see what abomination Julie has unleashed into the world.

13

YOUR CHANGING BODY

Physical Education

YOUR CHANGING BODY

Teen Health

By CLAUDE TUDETH

Educational Series

Bedtime Stories

Jenny's new Friends

ACTIVITIES FOR CHILDREN

Let's Summon Demons

CAN YOU GUESS

Who's Possessed Johnny?

HOW TO EXIT YOUR BODY
FOR BEGINNERS

Dr. PHIL McCOFFEN

Educational Series

HOW TO EXIT YOUR BODY

FOR BEGINNERS

by Dr. Phil McCoffen   72 pages

Jonah was sick of being told what to do. "Go to school! Look after your idiot brothers! Stop eating food that you find in the rubbish bin!"

But by mastering the secrets of **Astral Projection**, Jonah was free to go wherever he wanted. Imagine travelling to far away dimensions and galaxies, all from the comfort of your bedroom!

Let's face it, your physical body is weak, ugly, and smells funny. Free yourself from this fleshy prison in 12 easy-to-learn steps with this unique spiritual guide book.

You'll be happy to be sent to your room!

"Out-of-body experiences are often dismissed as a pseudoscience or even utter garbage," says author, Dr. McCoffen. **"But I beg you to buy my book! I'm broke, I need this!"**

~~$6.50~~   Only $4.95

EAT YOUR GREENS

HEALTH & NUTRITION

Sell Your Soul!

Economics for Children

B.M.HEX Gang

by Diane Rott   145 pages

An all-new adventure in the B.M.Hex Gang series!

After accidentally reading an incantation from an old book of witchcraft, Donna, April, and Caroline have invoked the worst of all demons—Satan himself!

The only way to banish the Dark Lord is to beat him in the BMX Championship race known as **"The DeathCourse."** But the Devil is a mean BMX freestylist, and the tournament is only one week away!

Will the B.M.Hex Gang be able to win the DeathCourse, save the town, and still have time to completely ruin the junior prom?

Nonstop action and suspense!

~~$4.95~~ **Only $3.95**

28

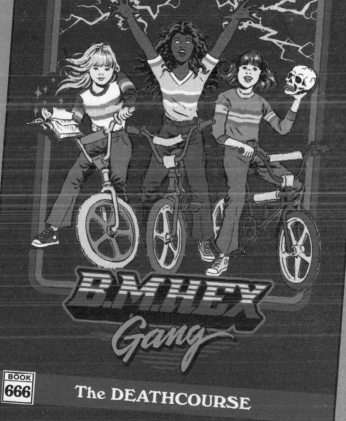

created by
DIANE ROTT

B.M.HEX
Gang

BOOK
666

The DEATHCOURSE

Tag,
You're It!

Hobbies
&
Games

GO TO HELL!

Patrick is a no-good sinner and must now spend eternity suffering horribly in Hell. Can you help him get there?

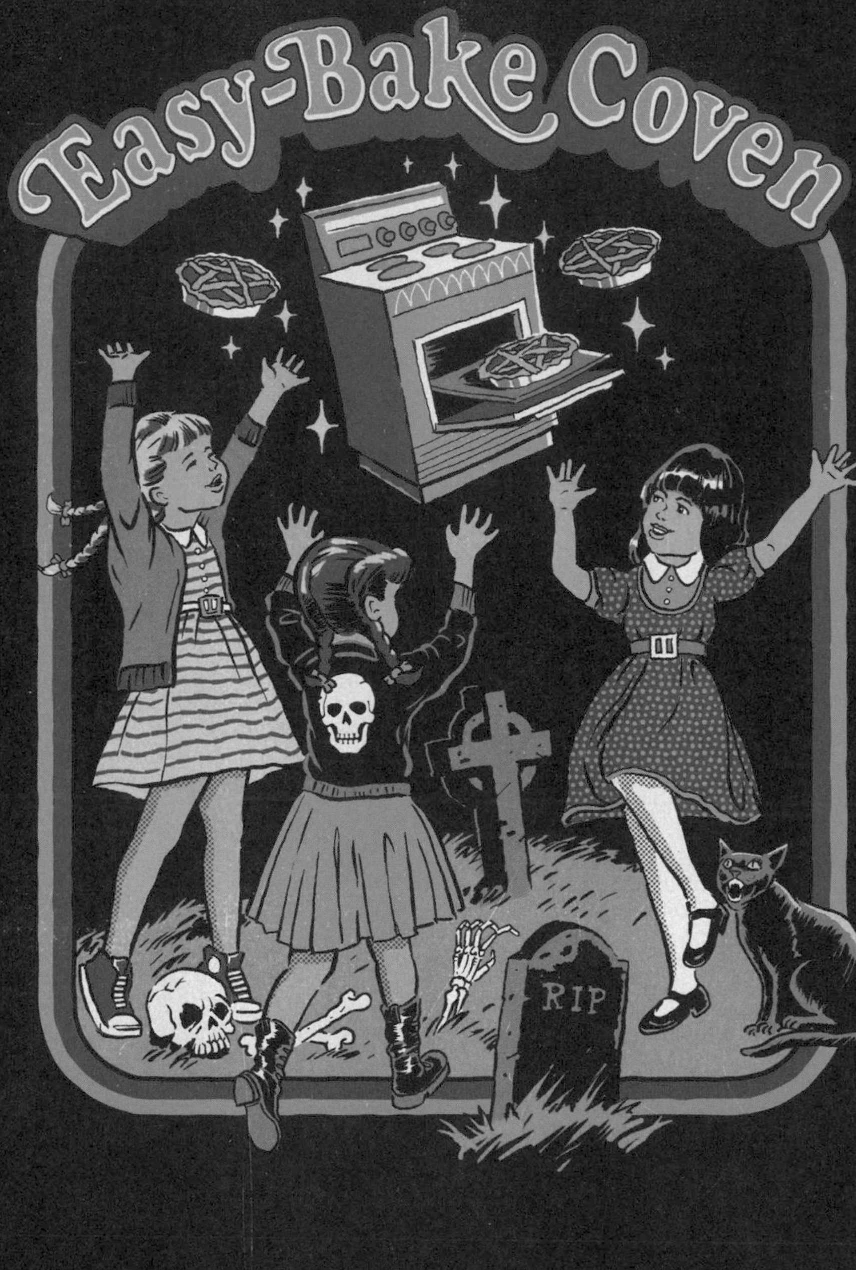
Easy-Bake Coven
RIP

My Little OCCULT Book Club

★ My ★ Favorite

Nursery Rhymes

Compiled by D. Monick

My ⭐ Favorite ⭐ Nursery Rhymes

Compiled by D. Monick   40 pages

**"Jack and Jill went up the hill
to fetch a pail of water,
The well was cursed,
they tell headfirst,
to vile and gruesome slaughter."**

Read along to all of your favorite
nursery rhyme classics with this
beautifully illustrated collection.
Includes *Mary Sacrificed a Little
Lamb*, *Baa Baa Black Magic*, and *Polly
Put the Cauldron On*.

Includes 12 bonus color stickers to
collect and trade!

~~$4.50~~   **$2.95**

Free Badge!

HAIL SANTA

This festive holiday badge is yours
FREE when you order!

Alien ABDUCTION Club

YES! I WOULD LIKE TO ORDER THE

ALIEN-ATTRACTING HELMET!

AS SEEN ON TV

THE ALIENS ARE COMING!

Wouldn't it be amazing to escape from your pointless existence of homework and chores and be swept light years across the galaxy?

With the secret technology contained within our **ALIEN-ATTRACTING HELMET,** you can! Send signals deep into space that invite any nearby extraterrestrials to come and pay you a visit. Who knows, they may even invite you onto their flying saucer! So what are you waiting for?
Order yours now!

CAUTION:
May cause extreme dizziness and baldness. Do not use if pregnant.

My Little **OCCULT** Book Club

MAIL COUPON TODAY!

MY LITTLE OCCULT BOOK CLUB
666 Doomsday Parade, Crypt Valley, USA

**Yes please send me a quantity of ....
ALIEN-ATTRACTING HELMET/S at
$13.95 each, plus $2 handling and
postage. Total enclosed: ....**

NAME ....

ADDRESS ....

CITY ....

STATE............... ZIP...........

IMPORTANT: Not all alien encounters have positive outcomes. Use at own risk.

Fun at the Farm

FIND A WORD

18 creepy words have been hidden in the jumble below.
Does Tony have the basic intelligence to find them?

```
D E X O R C I S M T A W A E
A E T E N C H A N T K I O O
G A M A Y M A T O L A T B X
T L W O Q U G A C Z C C N C
R P D V N S I N O A O H L U
T I C R Y P T A N E U C P R
A A T A A E I M J I A R A S
B Q E U A L B N U G R A V E
L I A V A L D A R B T F A P
O B H T O L I Z E A L T G N
O N E C R O M A N C Y D H Y
D E X S C H D V Q U A J O A
A I L W X A R O S L B I S Q
D O O M S D A Y O T J Y T P
```

43

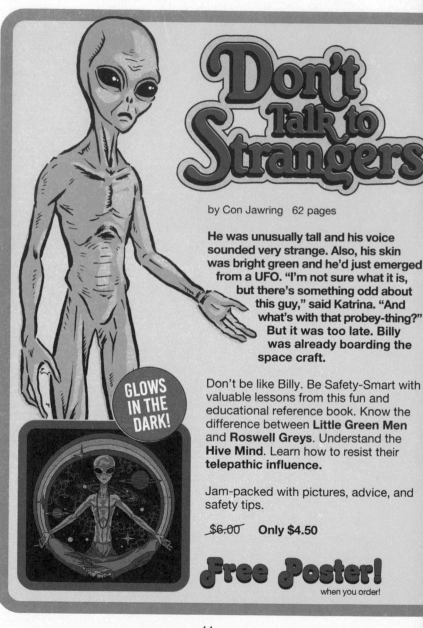
44

By Con Jawring

Life Skills SERIES

Don't Talk to Strangers

SAFETY EDUCATION

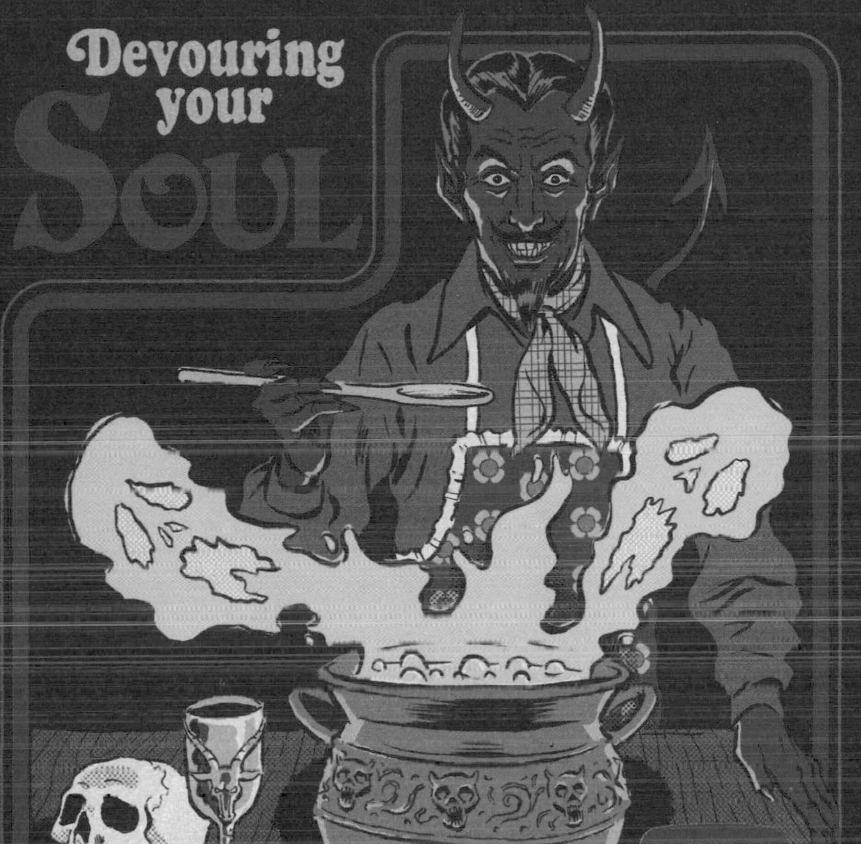
Devouring your
SOUL
AS SEEN ON
TV
Cook Book

Curses & Spells

FOR KIDS!

PAPER DOLL

Ken needs to get dressed for his busy day ahead, but he can't decide what to wear!

bone saw

cult robes

nuclear apocalypse

nail bat

sacrificial dagger

zombie outbreak

MY FIRST ZOMBIE APOCALYPSE

by Abbie Toir   34 pages

Well, it finally happened. The dead have risen from their graves and wander the earth, hungry for human brains!

Now it's up to Ritchie and his friends to hack, stab, and decapitate the zombie hordes before it's too late.

Sure, the world is now essentially an ash-covered graveyard and most of your friends have been brutally disembowelled, but don't let that deter you. Learn survival tips, innovative weapon-making, and beheading techniques with this colorful handbook for beginners.

20 full-color illustrations!

~~$4.50~~   **Now only $2.50**

Let's
Talk to Ghosts®

ABCDEFGHIJKLM
NOPQR STUVWXYZ
1234567890

NO   YES

ACTIVITIES FOR CHILDREN

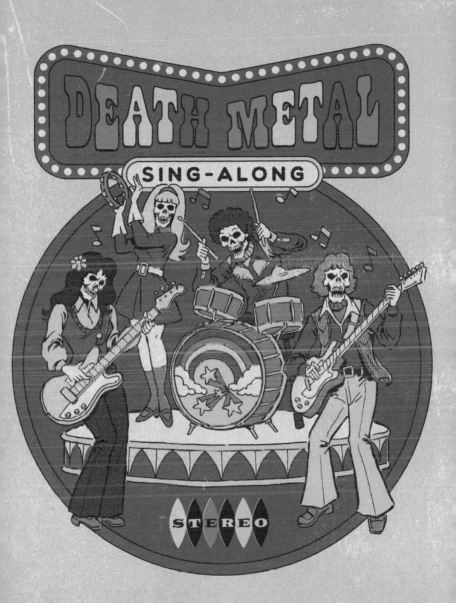

Bloody Mary

Caring for your HELL HOUND ©

Pets & Responsibilities

Caring for your Demon Cat©

Pets & Responsibilities

COLOR IN

Aliens are abducting the townsfolk. Are they taking them to share a higher wisdom about the potential of the human species, or will they simply harvest their organs for biofuel?

SHADOW PUPPETS

All you need to make these shadow puppets is a lamp, a blank wall, and an open mind.

THE DEVIL

BUTTERFLY

RABBIT

HORSE

63

ALL MIXED UP

Molly is going vampire slaying. Uh-oh! It looks like her equipment is all mixed up. Can you circle the items she should take with her?

kite

garlic

clock

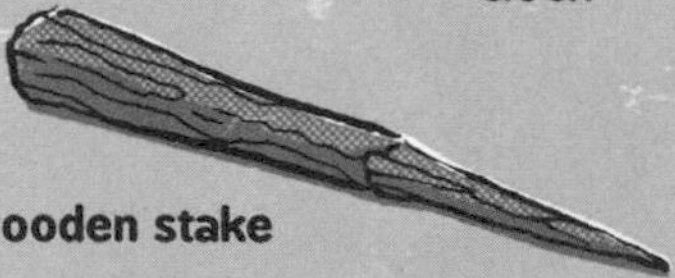

crucifix

wooden stake

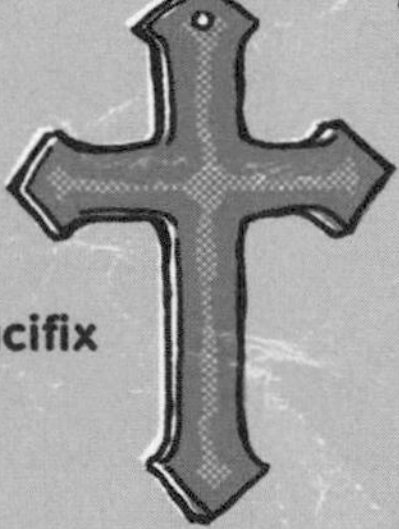

telephone

balloon

holy water

Let's Call the

Exorcist

My first

Alien Autopsy

ACTIVITIES FOR CHILDREN

HALLOWEEN
DOUBLE PACK

PUMPKIN'S REVENGE

A HALLOWEEN ADVENTURE

LOU SIFFER

WHO LIVES WHERE?

These 3 monsters have lost their way home.
Can you draw a line to show them where they live?

vampire

kennel

werewolf

sarcophagus

mummy

coffin

75

my imaginary friends

THINK I'M COOL

ODD ONE OUT

Katie the witch needs to choose a new familiar to assist with her dark bidding. Can you help her decide? But beware! One of these critters doesn't belong.

toad

duckling

black cat

crow

snake

spider

79

Steven Rhodes is a graphic artist and illustrator based in Brisbane, Australia. With designs such as *Let's Summon Demons* and *Pyrokinesis For Beginners*, you would be forgiven for thinking he has an affinity with the dark arts. In truth, Steven's iconic 'Sinister Seventies' collection was born from his dual love of retro nostalgia and pitch-black humor. His bestselling collections of shirts and merchandise are available in multiple retailers internationally, including Spencer's and Hot Topic. He spends his free time exploring vintage stores and not speaking to strangers.

Easy-Bake Coven (page 32), Let's Conjure Bloody Mary (page 54), and It Followed Me Home (page 55) appear courtesy of Creepy Company.

Library of Congress Cataloging-in-Publication Data

Names: Rhodes, Steven (Artist), author, illustrator.
Title: My little occult book club / Steven Rhodes.
Description: San Francisco : Chronicle Books, [2020]
Identifiers: LCCN 2019059933 | ISBN 9781797203256 (hardcover)
Subjects: LCSH: Book cover art—Parodies, imitations, etc.—Juvenile literature. | Books and reading—Parodies, imitations, etc.—Juvenile literature. | Paranormal fiction—Parodies, imitations, etc.—Juvenile literature. | Horror tales—Parodies, imitations, etc.—Juvenile literature. | Parodies—Juvenile literature. | LCGFT: Parodies (Literature) | Humor.
Classification: LCC NC973 .R46 2020 | DDC 741.6/4—dc23
LC record available at https://lccn.loc.gov/2019059933

Manufactured in China.

Design by Steven Rhodes and Neil Egan.

10 9 8 7 6 5 4 3

Chronicle books and gifts are available at special quantity discounts to corporations, professional associations, literacy programs, and other organizations. For details and discount information, please contact our premiums department at corporatesales@chroniclebooks.com or at 1-800-759-0190.

Chronicle Books LLC
680 Second Street
San Francisco, California 94107
www.chroniclebooks.com